Tuned Percussion

Pieces & Studies
for Trinity College London
exams from 2007

Grades 1-5

Published by
Trinity College London Ltd
trinitycollege.com

Registered in England
Company no. 09726123

Copyright © 2006 Trinity College London
Sixth impression, April 2023

Unauthorised photocopying is illegal
No part of this publication may be copied or reproduced in any
form or by any means without the prior permission of the publisher.

Printed in England by Halstan & Co, Ltd, Amersham, Bucks.

Trinity College London
Graded tuned percussion exams

Tuned Percussion Performance Notes

Playing tuned percussion successfully requires a relaxed and fluent approach throughout all the grades.

Control of the stick is based on developing a comfortable and practical grip. There are many versions of the fundamental grip but generally the stick should be held between the thumb and the first finger, resting in the curve of the finger joint. The other fingers curve round to give greater technical control. The palm faces down towards the instrument.

Mallets should be appropriate for the instrument. The student will not be able to make a good sound on any instrument if the mallet or stick used is unsuitable or of poor quality. Aim for good sound production including, at higher grades, a variety of tone colours.

Strokes should be fluent, using the wrist and fingers for greater articulation when needed. The note should always be struck in the centre of the bar over the resonator. Nodal (suspension) points should be avoided except for special effects. Sticking should be both practical and musical, using a hand-to-hand pattern, with double sticking used only when musically or technically necessary.

Rolls should be relaxed in nature with good movement in the wrist. It is very important to avoid tension in the arm. The roll should fit musically into the line of the music and keep the same dynamic as in the musical phrase. In early grades rolls may be rhythmically based, with the emphasis on fluency rather than speed.

Scales should be played hand-to-hand with a speed appropriate to the grade. Again, fluency and movement on the instrument is the main objective. Scales are important not just for acquiring technical control but also to help the player become a well-rounded musician with a secure sense of key. Movement between the lower and upper keyboards (naturals and accidentals) should be confident, led by a strong sense of knowledge of the key. The circle of fifths (given opposite) should be used as an aid to understanding how key patterns work and their relationship to one another.

Confident physical movement up and down the instrument will increase accuracy and fluency. The stance should be relaxed, with knees slightly bent to avoid tension. The neck should not be bent forward but should allow easy movement of the eye from instrument to music and back. Awareness and use of peripheral vision should be encouraged at the earliest opportunity. Moving the eye between music and instrument aids good reading practice and builds confidence. This leads naturally to including the conductor as a third peripheral vision element for the student in an ensemble context. Body language and the relationship between the player and the instrument are vitally important to playing in higher grades. Establishing this at lower grades will encourage confident playing.

Circle of Fifths

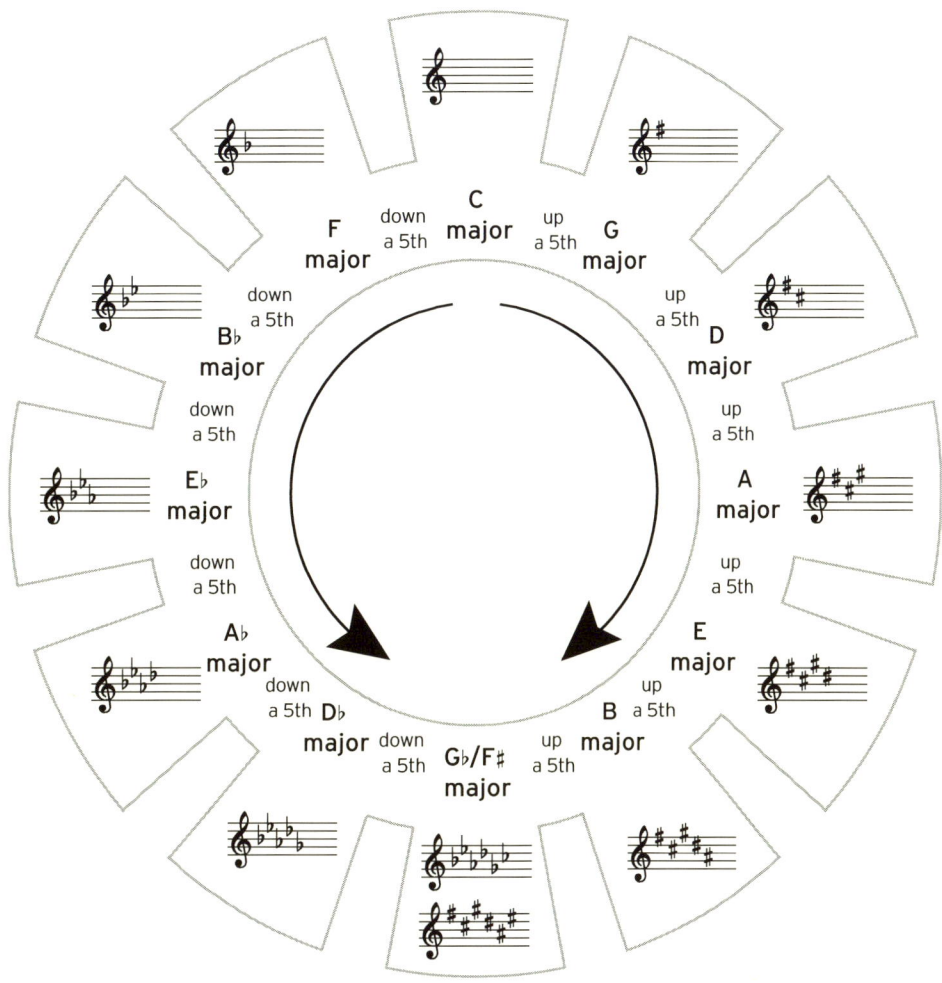

Walking Along

Jan Faulkner

Andante ♩ = 100

Oranges and Lemons

This Old Man

Grade 1 Major Study

Play this study steadily and with a confident sound.

Jan Faulkner

Grade 1 Minor Study

Where there is double sticking, float the hand from note to note giving a relaxed feel.

Jan Faulkner

GRADE 2

Hi Five!

Jan Faulkner

A version of this piece for timpani and piano can be found in the *Timpani Grades 1–5* book published by Trinity. The piece can be played as a duet with tuned percussion and timpani.

Copyright © 2006 Jan Faulkner

In the Clouds

Jan Faulkner

Rumba

Jan Faulkner

Up and Down

Jan Faulkner

Copyright © 2006 Jan Faulkner

Hickory Dickory Dock

Traditional
arr. Jan Faulkner

Grade 2 Major Study

This study should be played *mf* throughout. Feel the 6/8 pulse and follow the phrase marks.

Jan Faulkner

Copyright © 2006 Jan Faulkner

Grade 2 Minor Study

This study should be played in a confident manner with well contrasted dynamics.

Jan Faulkner

Copyright © 2006 Jan Faulkner

GRADE 3

Flamenco

Jan Faulkner

Repeat must be played in the exam.

On the Breeze

Jan Faulkner

Grade 3 Major Study

This study should be played precisely and with attention to rhythmic detail.

Jan Faulkner

Tuned Percussion

Pieces

for Trinity College London
exams from 2007

Grades 1–5

Piano accompaniments

Published by
Trinity College London Press Ltd
trinitycollege.com

Registered in England
Company no. 09726123

Copyright © 2006 Trinity College London
Sixth impression, April 2023

Unauthorised photocopying is illegal
No part of this publication may be copied or reproduced in any
form or by any means without the prior permission of the publisher.

Printed in England by Halstan & Co, Ltd, Amersham, Bucks.

GRADE 1

Walking Along

Jan Faulkner

Copyright © 2006 Jan Faulkner

GRADE 1

Oranges and Lemons

Traditional
arr. Jan Faulkner

GRADE 1

This Old Man

Traditional
arr. Jan Faulkner

Hi Five!

Jan Faulkner

Copyright © 2006 Jan Faulkner

Rumba

Jan Faulkner

Up and Down

Jan Faulkner

Hickory Dickory Dock

Traditional
arr. Jan Faulkner

In the Clouds

Jan Faulkner

[Blank page to facilitate page turns]

GRADE 3

Flamenco

Jan Faulkner

Repeat must be played in the examination.

On the Breeze

Jan Faulkner

Charlie is My Darling

Traditional
arr. Jan Faulkner

Tango

Jan Faulkner

Czardina

Jan Faulkner

Hi Five! for Four

Jan Faulkner

Grade 3 Minor Study

This study is for roll preparation and should be played with hard beaters.

Jan Faulkner

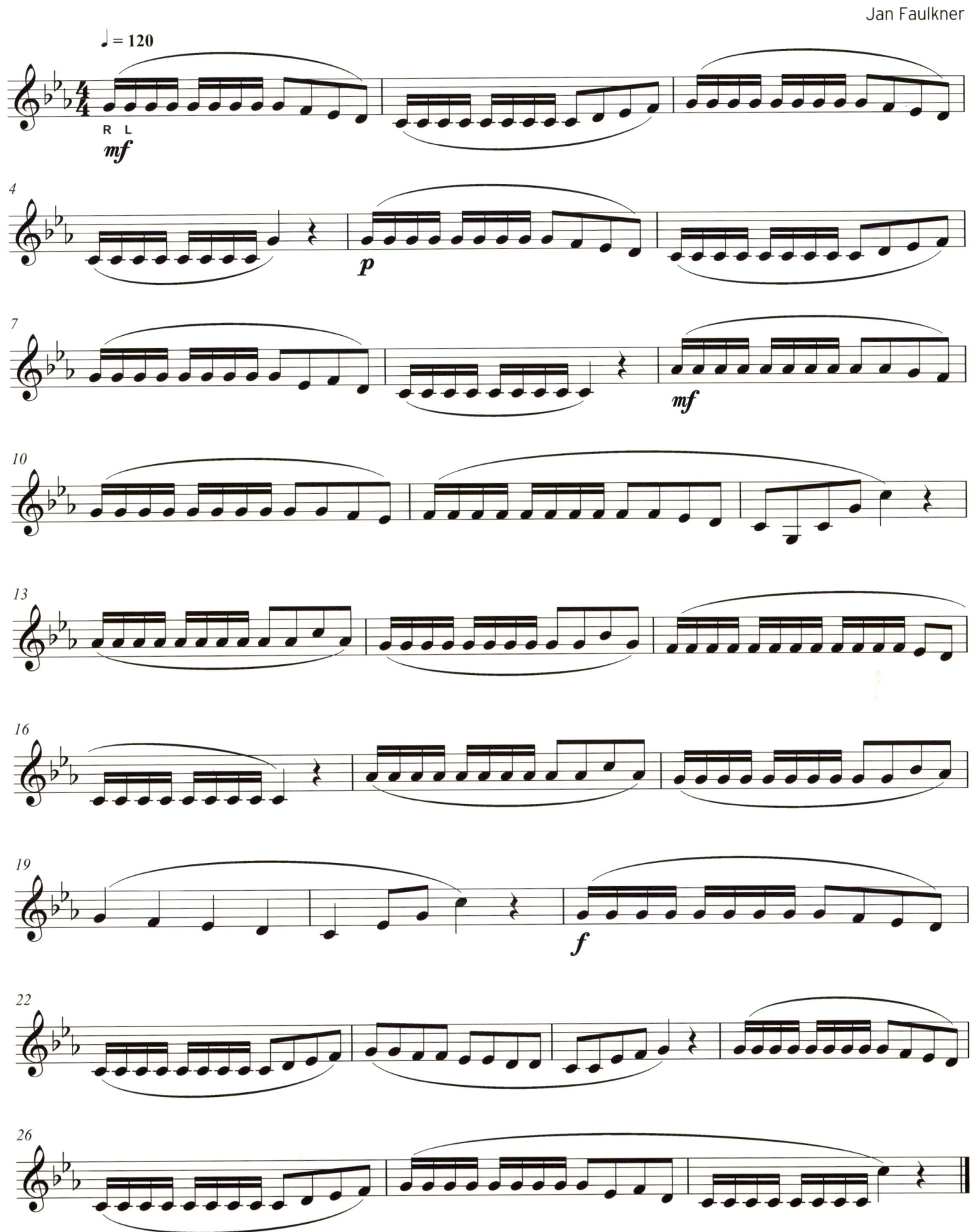

Charlie is My Darling

Traditional
arr. Jan Faulkner

Tango

Jan Faulkner

Grade 4 Major Study

This study should be played with a light touch. The phrasing and stickings should be adhered to.

Jan Faulkner

Copyright © 2006 Jan Faulkner

Grade 4 Minor Study

This study is to promote a steady sense of pulse within a fluent melodic line.
Rolls should be relaxed and should fit the line of the phrase.

Jan Faulkner

Czardina

Jan Faulkner

Hi Five! for Four

Jan Faulkner

Grade 5 Major Study

Think in 2 throughout this study and let the syncopations lie within the pulse.

Jan Faulkner

Grade 5 Minor Study

This study promotes independence of the hands. Really 'sing' the melody and observe the tenuto markings.

Jan Faulkner

Copyright © 2006 Jan Faulkner